Oswiecim: C
Into The Cam

Book 2 of
Auschwitz: Frozen Memories of the Concentration Camps

By Polish Underground Survivors

American History X Editor
World War 2 Publishing
Holocaust Photos Illustrator

All Rights Reserved. No part of this publication may be reproduced in any form, by any means, including scanning, photocopying, or otherwise without the prior written consent from the copyright holder.
Special Amazon Edition 2015

Copyright

Table of Contents

CHAPTER 1 3
ROUND UP 3
CHAPTER 2 7
CATTLE CAR 7
CHAPTER 3 14
GYMNASTICS 14
CHAPTER 4 20
"WORK BRINGS FREEDOM!" 20
CHAPTER 5 25
THE GHOST BATTALION 25
CHAPTER 6 35
GOLGOTHA 35
CHAPTER 7 37
THE DOGS OF WAR 37
CHAPTER 8 41
PURGATORY CHAMBER 41
CHAPTER 9 46
TEN FOR ONE 46
CHAPTER 10 49

HIDE - AND – SEEK	49
CHAPTER 11	52
JAN'S ESCAPE	52
CHAPTER 12	58
OTHER SOURCES	58
HOW TO CONTACT THE AUTHOR	68

Chapter 1

ROUND UP

"ALL INTO THE TRUCKS!" barked the Nazi officer.

My friend, Jan Jaworski, and I had been standing on Solec Street talking when the two German trucks drove up and stopped. We had sensed trouble of some sort, although there was no particular cause for alarm at first. The driver of one of the trucks got out and fumbled with the motor. We watched him. Suddenly we had become aware that there were uniformed Gestapo men all around us, herding together all those who happened to be on the street.

We started to run. The trucks blocked the street. We ran in the other direction. Trucks and Gestapo men were there, too. A machine gun was already set up at the intersection.

The hunters had trapped us.

That was the way it happened to us that August morning in 1940. What we had feared most ever since the Germans first occupied Warsaw had come about. "This is the end," I mumbled to myself. "What a way to have it happen," said an old man at my elbow, echoing my thoughts.

Panic began to spread among us... What about our families! Have they too been caught! How can we get word to them!

"Step along — you swine!" snarled the Gestapo man.

We were pushed into trucks and driven toward Praga. Rumors flew fast among those of us in the truck. "It's only a routine checkup, "offered Jan hopefully, who always took the optimistic point of view.

"They're taking us to do temporary work on the barracks in the suburbs," someone else volunteered. "No, it's for building fortifications," countered a third.

But the more the theories, and the more emphatically their sponsors argued, the more apparent it became that none of us knew why we had been snatched from the streets, where we were going, or when, if ever, we would return.

The more practical ones in the truck were writing notes on scraps of paper and furtively dropping them out on the street, hoping they would be picked up and delivered to the addresses scribbled on them.

The truck stopped at a large warehouse on Skaryszewska Street in Powisle. Inside we were lined up for examination. The officer on duty explained nothing as he looked over our identification papers. To Jan and me he said, "Remain!" He pointed to the line on his right, where most of the helpless herd eventually found itself. To a few he said, "Free." Such was the good fortune of a hospital employee, a streetcar operator, a gas worker and several others from my neighborhood whom I recognized. Whim, rather than occupation, age or physical appearance, seemed to decide whether a man went free or was condemned to slavery.

All day we stood and waited. All day new truck loads of human freight were delivered to the warehouse — men from all over Greater Warsaw, from Wola, Mokotow, Zoliborz, from all the outskirts and from the very heart of the city, thousands of them —rounded up like animals, raw material for the Nazi war machine.

As evening brought it's usual coolness we shivered in our light clothing. All through the night the examination of papers dragged on, while we tossed about restlessly on the warehouse floor.

With the second day came thirst that clouded the mind and impatient hunger in bodies already undernourished by ersatz food. That afternoon we were transferred to an old riding academy on Lazienkowska Street. Apparently the number of victims had been predetermined, for here the final selection was made, while we shuffled back and forth through the manure that covered the flooring.

Finally, after more hours of anxious waiting and bitter hunger, we were again loaded into trucks.

"Where to this time?" We all wondered.

Chapter 2

CATTLE CAR

WE soon found out. The trucks took us to a railroad siding. There we were herded into cattle cars that were immediately sealed. Someone murmured "Oswiecim" and everyone groaned. We all knew what that meant. "The camp of death," said Wladyslaw Zajac, the apprentice printer, "the camp from which no one returns alive."

"But they let you write," spoke up Jan hopefully.

"Yes," sneered Zajac, "there's only one thing they ever let you write—'I am well'. That's the one official message. That's all they'll ever hear from you from Oswiecim."

"And I knew a woman," continued another man, "who got a card like that from her husband in Oswiecim and the next day his ashes arrived in a tin box."

"The only time our friends will ever know the truth about us is when our families put the official notice in the Nowy Kurier Warszawski:—'The Requiem Mass for the soul of the late X. Y. will be celebrated tomorrow. The funeral will take place after the arrival of the ashes of the deceased.'

""They don't say 'ashes' in the notices anymore — not since everyone learned that that always meant Oswiecim."

"But they don't kill everyone at Oswiecim, do they?" asked a young lad of eighteen in a quavering voice.

Nobody answered. Nobody knew and nobody wanted to think about it.

The cattle car jerked and started to move. Every foot it moved tugged at our hearts — our hearts in Warsaw. A lot of the men were crying. Those of us who had been unable to write notes from the trucks were feeling desperate now about notifying our families. An acquaintance of mine, Jozef Karpowicz, noticed a man standing in a corner with a toolbox.

"Hey carpenter," he said in a low voice, "what you got in that box?"

"My tools."

"Got anything that will bore a hole?"

The carpenter said he did.

"Good!" replied Karpowicz. "We'll bore a hole in the side of the car and drop a message on the tracks. Quick — we'll be coming to the yards in a few minutes.

There are always men working on the tracks in the yards."

We all jumped to the idea and began writing notes. Meanwhile Karpowicz and the carpenter worked out the scheme very cleverly. First they took the wooden handle out of a hammer, split it and hollowed out a deep groove in which the messages were compressed. Then the handle was bound together and stuck back in the hammer.

"Do you think the messages will be delivered?" I asked. "Even though the hammer is found by a Pole, were asking a lot of his patriotism to deliver messages all over the city, even to Praga, Powisle and other suburbs."

"Whoever he is — we'll give him a reward, "said Karpowicz. So we took up a collection of thirty zlotys and attached the notes to the hammer together with a message, "To the Finder: Can you please get this to our family, we have beren seized by the Gestapo from Warsaw!"

Finally the carpenter bored a hole through the side wall of the car and dropped the hammer.

After this first bit of excitement there was nothing but the misery and tedium of the slow journey. The crawling movement of the train indicated that there were many other cattle cars, perhaps fifty. It looked like it would be a long hard trip.

Night came, but we were not cold because the car was so close and we were packed so tightly together, one sweating body next to another. Without light, air, rest, food or water, we were sustained only by the mystery of where we were being taken, the imminence of greater danger.

By morning we were completely worn out. Our insides were tied in knots. Besides, we were in agony for lack of sanitary relief.

But on and on the train puffed and pulled, while in each car a hundred odd men sat or stood in a human stable, breathing the stuffy, stinking air. In the course of the day several men in our car collapsed, among them Franciszek Suski, who belonged to my local union. Jan and I tried to revive him, but we were unable to because of the bad air.

Suddenly the train stopped. We could see through a crack that we were in an open field bordered by a thin row of bushes. From the end of the train came the sound of commotion. Then pistol shots.

"They're going to execute us," someone cried. I, too, thought that might be what was going on, but it was not the case. The shouting subsided and after waiting an hour or more the train started again.

Later, by the grapevine, we found out what had happened. It seems that in one of the rear cars they had managed to break open a door to get air. When the train stopped three men jumped out and tried to escape. The guards spotted them almost at once and the three prisoners ended their escape in a clump of bushes, their bodies nailed to the ground by bullets. The long delay after the shooting was due to the fact that the Nazis had gone to the nearest village, taken three peasants from their chores, driven them to the train and forced them into the same car from which the dead men had escaped. The boys from the village had refilled the quota of victims assigned to the cattle train. The locomotive resumed its panting.

The hours dragged on as in an unshakable bad dream. Somehow we endured — and I marveled at the powers of endurance of human flesh. I remarked on this to Jan, who took exception. "Despite human flesh," he said, "man is sustained by the spirit." And I must admit that he demonstrated his own theory, for he went through the ordeal better than most of us. At times he was even cheerful. But being in no mood to discuss metaphysics I must have dozed off — or lost consciousness — drugged by the torpor of the foul atmosphere and mesmerized by the constant clickety-clack of the wheels.

See Quotes From Eva Kor, Another Survivor, About The Cattle Cars In The Last Chapter.

Chapter 3

GYMNASTICS

"RUN! RUN!" shouted the guards.

At first I thought the Nazis had softened with human sympathy and were giving us a chance to stretch our legs.

"Gymnastic exercises for the new arrivals, "the Oswiecim receiving officer had curtly ordered when we landed at length in the camp we had all so greatly feared. I didn't know the significance of the officer's sinister inflection, nor did I suspect that "gymnastics" meant much worse suffering than riding forty-eight hours in a cattle car.

They brought us to the exercise yard, where we changed into prison clothing. We were broken up into groups, each forming a big circle. Then we were told to run — smartly and in formation.

The first lap felt good. It warmed my bare feet — they had us remove our sticky shoes. But on the second lap the hard gravel began to burn my soles. The third time around the circle it seemed like I was running on soft, green grass, but that was just the numbness coming into my feet, numbness that soon turned to sharp pain. Gravel, I learned, can scorch like the top of a red-hot stove.

"Run, run!" A hundred and fifty steps a minute on thousands of sharp needles that stabbed and jabbed. Some of the men began to waver. By slapping and beating them the guards kept them going.

I wondered if we were permitted to run outside the gravel path where the ground was softer. Others must have had the same idea, until one fellow, Michal Dombek it was, swerved out of the circle and was tripped up at once by a guard. He lay on the ground, bent up in agony, until the guard kicked him to his feet and pushed him back into the circle. We were getting our first exercise in German discipline!

"Run, run!"—Like the clickety-clack of the train, it seemed like the monotonous refrain of a dream.

One old man — one of the oldest in our circle — seemed to be making his last efforts to keep up with the merry-go-round. The guards had to whack him across the shoulders with a club to spur him on. His face turned dark. But somehow he managed to keep picking up his feet and putting them down again on the jagged stones.

Gradually the brown gravel took on the color of human blood — first a pale pink, then red, then purple stones that already had been dyed with many coats of human pigment.

My body became a mass of throbbing nerves. Every breath I took plunged a long blade into my breast. My head hammered incessantly, keeping time with the endless pounding of heavy feet on the purple gravel and with the constant "Run, run!" of the guards — the dirge of Oswiecim.

Several of the men, including Jan, lost consciousness — but not for long. Jan was revived by being dragged over to a pump, where they poured water over him until he got onto his feet and came back to the exercises. Others seemed to require more forceful treatment. One they brought to by stamping on his chest with their heavy boots. Back he went into the circle. Another, who did not respond to that method, was brought back to his senses by a guard who jammed a stick in his mouth and twisted it. There was no escape from "Run, run!"

To relieve their boredom the guards introduced a new routine:—"Halt! About face! Run! "The idea of this was to produce dizziness, nausea and more unconscious victims to pummel. Each time I turned around the faces of my fellow gymnasts seemed to be whirling in a fantastic dance. Even the red barrack blocks in the background seemed to join in the kaleidoscopic ballet.

The last exercise turned out to be an ingenious form of torture.

"Halt!" cried a guard. "Squat on the knees. Do not move until the order is given."

How long we had to stay in the squatting position I cannot say, it seemed so eternal. My muscles trembled violently. My torn feet could not support the weight of my body and my knees shook; I could not control them. All of us were the same — legs wobbling, faces pale with pain and anger. The guards roared with laughter at the grotesque exhibition. A blow on the shaking knees was intended to steady them and bring the prisoner to order. "Keep positions! Failure to obey orders will be punished."

They waited until a dozen or more of us collapsed completely before ending their little initiation to Oswiecim.

"Attention! March to the barracks!"

I pulled together what was left of my body and dragged myself gratefully to the barracks that were tracked with bloody stains.

Once inside, we tried to do something about our feet. There was nothing we could find for bandages. Our prison suits could not be torn up. We did find some scraps, of paper, but the blood soaked through it quickly.

"You're wasting your time," said a camp veteran of six months. "Wounds never heal in Oswiecim."

I was to learn how truthfully he spoke. For "gymnastics" was not just for newcomers. It was part of the daily routine. And tomorrow the foot wounds would deepen and the next day they would begin to fester and become fetid, and the stains on the gravel would gradually change to the repulsive, nondescript color of wounds that never heal.

Himmler was in large part responsible for the torture techniques in the Concentration Camps. See Last Chapter For an Excerpt.

Chapter 4

"WORK BRINGS FREEDOM!"

THE official slogan of Oswiecim was Arbeit Macht Frei—"Work Brings Freedom." It was lettered on a big sign that hung over the camp entrance.

The symbol of our colony was a huge chimney painted bright red — the chimney of the crematory, which came to be known to us as "The Factory."

Between the sign and the chimney the life of every prisoner was suspended — from the moment he "gave up" his life on entering the camp until he regained it as a handful of ashes from the crematory. That was the only "freedom" our labors would bring us. For thousands of Polish labor slaves "Work Brings Freedom" was their epitaph, spelled out daily in the smoke from the Factory.

That was the most important product of Oswiecim — the smoke from the chimney, since the camp existed for the purpose of liquidating Polish lives. Fifty a day was a good "production" average. Every day the casket cart made regular trips to the crematory. On the return trip it brought back empties for refill.

Oswiecim had an economic program based on maximum "turnover" of labor. Everything went at top speed, whatever we did, wherever we worked. To help maintain the German Army we ran farms, raised livestock, mined coal, constructed buildings, loaded and unloaded trains. When there was more manpower than work to be done, work was created by detailing one group to cart sand from one place to another, and a second group to cart it back. And always it was "Rush, Rush!"

The day began at four A. M. — before dawn, even before reveille was sounded on the big gong at the gate. For we had to get a head start in order to avoid penalties for lateness. We jumped from our pallets, pulled on our clothing, rushed to the latrines that were always occupied, splashed ourselves in the same bowl of water used by hundreds of others. If we hurried we might have sufficient time to grab a few mouthfuls of food — one bowl had to serve three prisoners—and to drink our acorn coffee, before it was time for roll call.

After that important ceremony we quickly formed into different groups according to the order of the day. Those detailed for work at the sawmill stood near the gong; those to make concrete lined up near the middle barracks. In another spot were grouped the men assigned to the mines and farther away those to work in the fields. Once accounted for, we marched to work to the gala strains of band music.

My first day in Oswiecim was typical. In the middle of the camp was an uneven rise of ground. My group was detailed to cart dirt from some distance away and level off the top of the plateau. A synthetic rubber plant was to be built there.

With our wheelbarrows we formed a continuous "production line" that moved faster and faster as the overseer stepped up the pace. On the downgrade it was all right, But it was about all a man could do to push his loaded wheelbarrow up the hill. After the first few trips each at a quicker tempo the slope seemed like a mountainside, the wheelbarrow like a five-ton truck.

My stooped body soon became cramped with fatigue. My hands were so stiff I could hardly keep my hold on the handles. The veins in my arms swelled up until they looked as though they would burst.

"Quicker, quicker," cried the overseer, striding along the line using his whip at random.

"Courage," whispered Jan behind me, praying for strength himself.

"If I can only make the top of the rise," I thought to myself each time I started upgrade. "If only I can make it — one step, two steps, three, four..." The deadweight of the wheelbarrow swayed from side to side — my numbed fingers could not control it. I am sure it would have toppled over and me with it, had I not seen what happened to others who gave into their exhaustion. The beatings they got was stimulant enough to give me that extra ounce of strength. Hour after hour it went on — faster and faster. My heart pounded in every part of my body.

Many wheelbarrows overturned that day. Many of my companions collapsed. Although that cut down the manpower, it seemed to please the Germans, it was all in line with policy — the workers had earned their "freedom."

Chapter 5

THE GHOST BATTALION

I HAD BEEN in Oswiecim but a few days when I observed the weirdest procession I had ever seen in my life. Unlike the rest of us who marched to our jobs with military precision, these prisoners — about a hundred and fifty of them —kept only a semblance of a line and made no attempt to follow the mechanical rhythm of the band. They staggered along like drunkards —heads lolling from side to side, eyes half closed, bodies swaying. Or like shadows, pitching first one way, then another. It was a dance macabre, a demoniacal pantomime. I could scarcely believe that they were human beings.

"Who are those men over there?" I asked of the man marching next to me, a former schoolteacher named Stefan Wilczynski. "Are they drugged — or what?"

He glanced at them and turned away quickly.

"The ghost battalion," he said grimly."

What does that mean — the ghost battalion?

Wilczynski just shook his head. But later I found out about them from others. It seems they were the "graduating class" of Oswiecim. They had been through all the hard labor courses, had survived the various tortures on the schedule for them. Now they had the honor of being assigned to "light work." Digging potatoes, for example. Of course light work called for less food, so they were placed on half rations. With this diet their weight dropped four to five pounds every few days.

At home every one of these men would have been a critical case in the hospital. Here their treatment consisted of digging potatoes. Oswiecim drained the last drop of blood and marrow from its victims. Clubs had to be used freely to keep the skeletons moving. "Hey there — don't go to sleep," the overseer would snort at them. In the fields the more feeble ones had to crawl on the ground from one potato hill to another—legs and backs were too weak to bend over; hands were the only motive power left.

Every day a few more found their way to the building with the tall chimney. Every day a few more took their place in the Parade of the Living Dead.

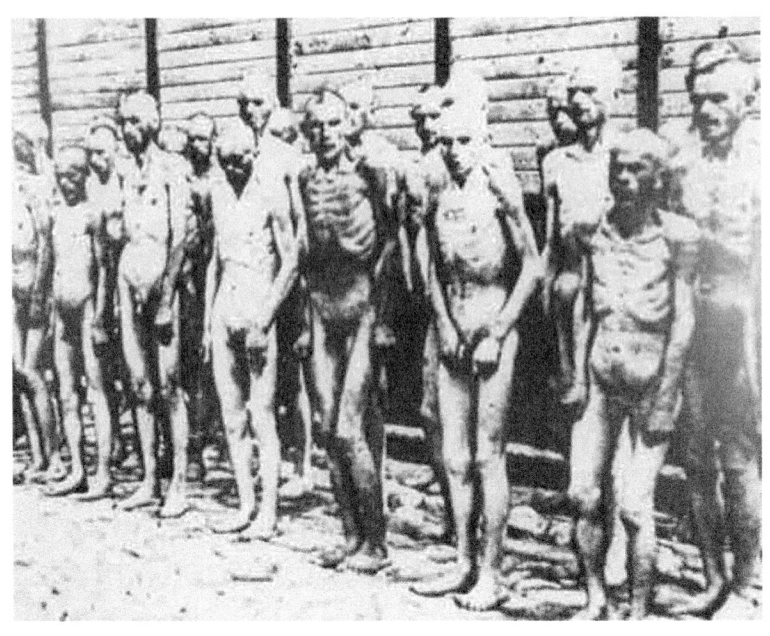

NO NIGHT IN OSWIECIM

HOW I longed for sleep those first few nights in Oswiecim! How little I got! My pallet of straw had been threshed a thousand times by the twisting bodies of former tenants, until now there was nothing left but chaff. I should have said "our" pallet — Jan's and mine — for each mattress was shared by two or more prisoners.

There was only one paper thin blanket to cover both our bodies, gripped with cold and trembling with fatigue. But over every one in that bare barrack room was a blanket of darkness in which pain, anxiety, nostalgia and fear blended together and lost their identity. Sleep would have given us all a few hours of escape, but only whispering relieved our suffering from work and punishment. Whispers that sounded like our own nightmares, unearthly voices that had no human relationship.

One whisperer in the night — my first night in camp — was a former exile to Siberia under the Czarist regime, one Kazimierz Zembrzuski. He told a long rambling story about a prison revolt, when a fellow inmate was beaten by a guard, about the ensuing trial, the legal defense, the verdict. But Zembrzuski's tale fell flat. Now and then one of the prisoners would laugh or interrupt with a brutal "Shut up!" After all, a description of Siberian exile was not to be compared with Oswiecim. His story was for children.

We were all glad when he was finally stopped by the Stubenfuehrer, the fellow-prisoner put in charge of our room, who snarled "Silence!" from his bed on top of the table.

Not always did the Stubenfuehrer stop the whispering, for even he liked to listen to an interesting tale that would for a few minutes transport him away from Oswiecim, that would blot out its haunting specter and drug his debased soul that he had traded for better food and a comfortable bed.

Such a story was that told by Stanislaw Kupczyk, the sailor. The Stubenfuehrer lifted his head from the couch to catch every word and everyone listened so quietly the whispering became clearly audible throughout the room. It was a tale of a phantom odyssey.

A ship was sailing on an immense ocean to an unknown land.—That night the stars of a foreign sky looked down on those fifty prisoners huddling together for warmth on the barrack floor.—And then, at last, we landed on a magic island of exotic beauty. Luxuriant foliage rustled high over our heads — we felt the balmy fragrance of the soft languorous breeze and forgot the cold Polish highlands. The odyssey continued, shifting to another setting, another time. All the adventure and humor and sadness of a rich life were blended by the narrator into romantic images of another world. It was all quite mad, for Kupczyk was delirious — he was soon to be "matriculated" to the Factory. Using words he scarcely knew before, he resurrected and recreated a lifetime of fact and fantasy. The empty silence was filled with poignant visions of beauty, freedom and fulfillment — distant echoes of rapturous dreams.

The spell was broken by the wailing from a mattress near the window, where a young boy lay. Today this boy, Piotr he was called, had been flogged twenty-five times with a great rawhide whip. The blows had cut his skin in many places, torn his muscles, had even driven bits of clothing into the wounds. Now his back was a mass of raw sores. Feverish and restless, he kept tossing and rolling, bumping first his neighbor on the left, then on the right.

"Sleep, boy, sleep," Jan called out to him.

"He had enough sleep during roll call," some one else cruelly commented.

Jan had witnessed the beating and whispered the story to me. It seems this young lad had been unloading big 165-pound bags of cement from a freight car. When he finished his work he looked as though he would die on the spot, but somehow he dragged himself back to camp and here made the mistake of dropping down beside a shed and falling asleep. Piotr was missing at evening roll call until they searched him out and had him whipped as a reminder of his duty. The poor boy moaned all night. Sleep was impossible for him; his only wish was to die. But next morning he was up and in line for roll call with the rest of us, and back he went to the station to unload more freight cars.

From the pallet near the lockers I kept hearing a peculiar shuffling sound. "That's the fellow we call the Engineer," a neighbor whispered when I inquired. "He's moving his arms up and down to get the numbness out of his shoulders. They were practically dislocated yesterday while he was hanging from the punishment post. He was penalized for smoking — two hours on the post. They break it up in two one-hour periods a week apart, to make the punishment last longer. All last week he couldn't sleep and kept the rest of us awake. Looks like we're in for another week of it."

Back and forth, up and down shuffled the arms of the Engineer. I could sense that it was not just the physical pain that racked his body. It was also his feeling of frustration and defeat that choked him inwardly, the awareness and resentment that he as a scientific man would have of the utter senselessness of his condition and of those around him.

"Turn over," Jan signaled to me, nudging me in the back so he would have room to shift his position. As we turned each one down the line turned. The room was so crowded we had to move in unison.

I was not long in learning to identify the sounds in an Oswiecim barrack — the rhythmic groaning that accompanied the torment of festering wounds; the low murmuring of men who prayed through the night — Jan right next to me was one of these; the constant scratching of itching scabs; the weary sighs of disgust because of the ever-present fleas and lice, for these vermin persisted despite the official "lice hunts."

There were other sounds, too, a body crawling across other bodies, the swearing of those who were stepped on, the patter of feet on the bare wooden floor near the door—someone gripped with dysentery, which was universal throughout the camp, or a man suffering from kidney trouble and forced to make endless trips to the latrine.

Still I would try to sleep — one had to. But the fitful dozing that was the shabby substitute for sleep brought neither forgetfulness nor relaxation.

Even the nights at Oswiecim granted no relief.

Chapter 6

Golgotha

Some weeks later, after Jan had been punished on the post like the Engineer, I found out more about this twentieth-Century form of inquisition. Jan pointed out the windows in the loft over the penal barrack. Inside I could barely make out the outlines of the roof pillars. It was from these posts that the men were suspended an hour at a time. Each post was always occupied; there were never any vacancies.

Jan told me what it was like. "They put your arms over your head," he said, "and then chain your wrists to hooks driven in the posts. You are hooked up to a height so that your feet just miss the floor. Your arms strain and stretch under the weight of your body until it seems as if they are pulled loose from their sockets. At first you twist and squirm to relieve the pressure on your wrists and shoulders, but every motion is agony. Each effort to rest your feet on the floor pulls you to pieces."

The worst of being "posted" was that after being chained up for an hour there was no way one could get relief, for regulations strictly forbade resting or sleeping in daytime. The unfortunate man had to drag his poor, aching body about the camp yard and surreptitiously lean against a barrack wall or stretch out on the ground. At night the thin pallet was scant protection from the hard floor and the next morning he would have to return to hard physical labor, regardless of swollen joints.

"Crimes" that led to the post could be almost any minor offense—smoking during work, hiding from work during a rainstorm, stealing bread, speaking out of turn at roll call.

Posting took place every Sunday. The idea of holding it in weekly installments instead of continuously followed out the Oswiecim principle of torturing a prisoner already condemned to death for months after sentence had been secretly passed.

Chapter 7

THE DOGS OF WAR

I NEVER used to be afraid of dogs — until I came to Oswiecim. Like most people I had thought of dogs as "man's best friend." But here we all learned to regard the dogs as our enemies, the same as their masters. Even the dogs had been poisoned with the Nazi doctrine of hate and cruelty.

My lesson came from personal experience. One of the dogs at the camp was a big, beautiful wolf dog that patrolled daily with his master on a route between the barbed wire fence of the main camp and the service buildings. The dog was perfectly trained, obedient to the slightest command. It walked at heel, sat down when his master stopped, jumped high when the signal was given him by hand, retrieved articles when commanded. His master, Hans Fischer, was a handsome young Nazi, who wore a meticulously neat, close-fitting SS uniform. How deceiving were his boyish complexion and innocent smile!

One day Fischer noticed me as I was struggling with a big pail of water. This was after I had been greatly weakened by two months' internment. My weight had dropped from a hundred and fifty to barely a hundred pounds, and after lugging the 20-pound bucket for half a mile I was exhausted. Of course I knew better than to try to stop and rest. But I did slow down and Fischer noticed that. To me he said nothing; to the dog he merely whispered, "Attack."

The animal lunged for me. He knocked me down and sank his teeth in my thigh. Instinctively I covered my head with my hands and screamed with terror — I knew the dog would go for my throat next.

Fischer was satisfied he had taught me a lesson, so he called the dog back and stroked his head. "Good work, old boy, good work," he said.

Meanwhile I struggled to my feet and went on with the water — this time at the official double-quick tempo, my leg streaked with blood. Like my bruised feet, the wound, I knew, would get worse in days to come. Another wound that would never heal!

My experience with the patrol dogs was not unique. Incidents similar to mine happened many times a day. There was one which was particularly revolting. A sudden heavy shower had clogged the camp sewer system so that it overflowed the yard. The sewer had to be drained by pails of water passed along a line of men to a drainage ditch. Several prisoners had to stand in the sewer with water up to their waists.

Standing over them were two guards with their dogs. The Nazis apparently thought this would be a good occasion to have a little fun. So at a sign one of the dogs pounced on the back of Tadeusz Michalski and grabbed at his throat. Then, a split second before the dog sank his fangs into the flesh, the guard called the dog back and patted him in appreciation.

This was repeated in a few minutes with another prisoner, then a third, until all had been used as practice dummies not once, but many times. When a man's weakened frame would buckle under the weight of the dog -— as frequently happened — the guards would shout with glee.

The excited dogs understood the game very well and, barking loudly, begged for a chance to attack another "enemy." For the guards it was fine training; they acquired new skill in maintaining the suspense of horror, in learning when to give the order to attack and the split-second moment to stop.

Meanwhile the prisoners bailed water at top speed, their faces covered with the sweat of fear, never knowing when a "mistake" would occur and one of the dogs would drive its teeth into their throats.

Chapter 8

PURGATORY CHAMBER

THE most closely guarded secret in Oswiecim was the underground penal chamber—some spoke of it as the "Purgatory Chamber." We knew many who went there, but none who ever returned.

The building itself was innocent in appearance. It was the corner block formed by the rectangle of prison barracks and, save for one difference, it was just like all the others—the same box-like shape, the same dreary red walls, designed in the style reminiscent of Austrian days, when barracks were built to house regiments of the Imperial Artillery. The sole architectural deviation of the penal barrack was the row of tiny fear, never knowing when a "mistake" would occur and one of the dogs would drive its teeth into their throats round windows that were set just above the ground. The windows lent a mysterious quality to the structure. It was as if they were the sightless eyes of the condemned men, straining for one last ray of light from the outside world.

But what went on inside the purgatory chamber? What new refinements of sadism awaited us there? How would we meet our end? There was much speculation about these matters so intimately connected with our personal destinies—since it was the "last stop" in Oswiecim for all of us — but we never had any real information until we stumbled upon the answer.

One day in October the entire group in Purgatory — about three hundred men — was moved out en masse to the hospital. Of course that was where they belonged anyway, but it was not because they were sick that they were removed. We could not understand why.

Then during the night we heard the crunching of feet on the gravel and the sounds of steps filtering down and vanishing into the basement. We counted five hundred lost souls on their "descent into hell."

"Who are they?" was the one question whispered around the barrack that night.

Every one was on edge to know how it could be that five hundred men healthy enough to march were going into the death chamber. It was the Stubenfuehrer himself who explained the identity of the new purge victims — "Russian prisoners of war." So now we had a new element in our transient population, which was largely Polish with a sprinkling of Czechoslovaks, Germans and Yugoslavs.

We all continued to listen closely for further activity. We did not have long to wait after the shuffling feet had ceased. Then came the shrieking—inhuman cries that pierced the night, penetrating the heavy walls of the lethal chamber.

They were cries of fear. I recognized them at once, for like my fellow colonists I had become expert in distinguishing cries of pain from those of fear or from those of despair and resignation. Several times the cries rose and fell in the night. Then at last nothing but utter silence, ominous silence that seeped through our souls. "God help them," whispered Jan to himself.

Next morning as I glanced furtively at the penal barrack it seemed like a huge mausoleum.

For three days there was no activity around the purgatory chamber. During the fourth night there was again the sound of crunching gravel. Carts were being brought up by special details to remove the clothing of the Polish prisoners who had been removed to the hospital. Next the carts picked up the Russians' uniforms, which were taken to the camp warehouse for repair and reconditioning. Finally they came for the corpses.

Jan, who had been assigned to the removal detail as a sort of minor punishment, later told me about it. Even he, the imperturbable Jan, was shaken by his harrowing experience for days, although dead men were common sights in Oswiecim. It was not just the corpses themselves, he said, it was the mute eloquence with which they cursed this gigantic outrage against all mankind. And it was the eerie setting, too —the feeble moonlight threw a ghastly floodlight over the stacks of stiffened limbs and livid flesh. The detail worked hard, laboriously wheeling the carts from the Purgatory to the crematory, to be finished with the job as quickly as possible.

On one trip, Jan told me, his cart overturned and the corpses rolled down an embankment, seeming to regain life for a few seconds as they clambered over each other, waving their sprawling arms and finally coming to rest in a scattered mass.

He and his mates worked feverishly to reload the cart in the fast disappearing darkness of night. The first rays of dawn streaked across the bodies of the dead and brought out an extraordinary greenish pallor in them. And then, in that, strange luminosity, Jan discovered the secret of Purgatory and of five hundred dead Russians. He had a corpse by the arm and suddenly he stopped and stared into its face. "My God!" he screamed, dropping the body and burying his head in his hands. Years ago—in 1917—he had seen that same spectral appearance when he came across a dead soldier in an abandoned trench.

It was the mark of poison gas.

Chapter 9

TEN FOR ONE

"THE SIREN!"

Its ominous wail could be heard by all for miles around as warning that a prisoner had escaped. To us it was more — it was the knell of death, for the camp rule provided that ten prisoners be held hostage for every escaped prisoner and that they be put to death in the event he was not captured.

The instant the siren sounded we all dropped what we were doing and rushed to the yard for roll call. It became a familiar Oswiecim routine. There we stood, paralyzed with fright, our eyes searching up and down the rows to find the missing one. Not that it would do us much good to know, for the terrible anxiety would remain until the ten hostages were picked.

Motionless we stood for one, two, three hours—on and on. From the West dark clouds approached with the night. Meals, sleep, everything was suspended, while the chill wind tore at our flimsy wood-fibre uniforms. Backs ached, legs ached, feet ached — and always the cold and the suspense.

Now and then the guard would turn his back. Quickly we waved our arms, shifted our feet, stretched our necks — like a mass convulsion sweeping our ranks. But we had to watch sharply, ready to stiffen to attention the instant the guard turned back.

Once in a while a body would fall to the ground, one prisoner was no longer concerned with whether he would or would not be one of the ten; now he had become the eleventh—or the first. It happened thus to Stefan Hrynkiewicz in my group. Since no one might move him, his body grew stiff in the wind, cold and rain of a twelve-hour vigil.

Other bodies would collapse and lose interest in the death watch.

Finally the Commandant would appear, pacing up and down the ranks. He strode silently, but the eyes of every man were fixed on his every movement. As the Commandant's eyes fell on each prisoner, he would straighten himself to the utmost, stick out his chest and raise his head, to look as healthy and valuable a piece of property as possible.

"Komm.'" fell the verdict softly, and the victim's body would make a final vain effort to convince the Commandant of his indispensability.

"Komm!" echoed the verdict harshly, and the prisoner's body deflated.

On moved the Commandant along the line.

Each time he chose a hostage, an inaudible sigh of relief went up from the rest of us.

The ten hostages were marched to the penal barrack, down the ten steps to Purgatory. Though the camp law provided for their release if the escaped prisoner was found in three days, they knew it was useless to hope. Even if the unlucky one was captured, both he and the hostages would be "processed" in Purgatory just the same.

Oswiecim knew no Resurrection.

Chapter 10

HIDE - AND – SEEK

UNLIKE those in some camps, the inmates of Oswiecim did not encourage each other to escape. The cruelty with which the ten-for-one law was enforced was unfortunately successful in appealing to their self-interest and in developing a moral code among the prison population that mercilessly condemned any one who would bargain with their lives as the price of his freedom.

Little as we valued our lives in Oswiecim, and as frequently as we tried to do away with them, somehow there remained enough primitive instinct for self-preservation to make us struggle against death as hostages and to regard the escape-minded prisoner as a social menace. That, together with our intense jealousy of anyone lucky enough to get away, put us in the ironical position of applying greater vigilance in the matter of escape than the guards themselves. Naturally the Nazis traded on this state of mind to the utmost.

One tragic incident demonstrated how thoroughly the "Oswiecim process" had debauched our mentality and character.

A crew of twenty prisoners was tearing down a building near the main road. Some of the men were smashing in the front walls with crowbars, others were carting away the debris and some were piling up the usable lumber. The guard was pleased with the men because they were fairly green and had not yet acquired the prison tricks of faking work.

Only one of them behaved like a veteran. He kept appearing in a different spot in the wreckage carrying the same piece of lumber. The guard soon suspected what he was planning to do. He watched him carefully but without making a move, so the prisoner became bolder. He put down his load and disappeared from view, but the guard spied him wriggling under a pile of rubbish. Giving him a few moments to get well out of sight, the guard raised his voice in a hoarse shout of alarm:

"Wojcik has escaped! Quick — look for him!"

Instantly stampeded into action, the crew searched furiously among the debris. The Nazi, assuming the role of beater in the hunt, directed them first one way and then another, to buildup the suspense of the sport as long as possible, but always moving them gradually in the direction of the would-be runaway.

At last one of the crew uncovered the hiding man. He struck at him with a crowbar.

"Don't hit me," the captive begged. "You have found me. I won't escape again."

But his appeal for mercy went unheeded. One after another the prisoners rained blows on him, each seeking personal vengeance.

The guard was delighted with his little game of cops and robbers, until he realized it was about to end.

"Stop!" he called, bit it was to late.

A blow on Wojcik's head had ended his struggle, "freed" by the hands of his own brothers in suffering!

Chapter 11

JAN'S ESCAPE

AFTER all the horror and misery he had gone through, it was finally imagination that broke down my good friend, the optimistic Jan Jaworski.

It was because of one short phrase in a letter he received from his wife: —"I am so grateful that you have your own means of escape." That was all,—just those twelve words that condemned Jan to death — in his own mind.

I say it was his own imagination, but he knew the ways of the Nazis better than I did. Be that as it may, Jan was certain that he would be called before the Gestapo to "explain" that passage in his wife's letter and "reveal" his secret plan for escaping from Oswiecim. He felt it would be impossible to prove the innocence of that phrase to the cynical Nazis, and futile to try.

"The Gestapo just would not believe that she was only referring to man's spiritual powers of resistance to evil," he said hopelessly. "They could never understand that was why I have not cracked up as so many of the others have, that it was because I had something here"—placing his hand over his heart — "that could withstand any torture they might put me through. In their stupidity they would only suspect a crude plot of some kind. There's just no use trying to convince them."

"But Jan," I argued, "they haven't even questioned you yet. Maybe they did understand the meaning of the phrase. Or maybe they didn't even notice it. Why look for trouble until it comes?"

But there was no reasoning with him. Jan, the optimist, had suddenly become the gloomiest of pessimists. That was the way it often happened in Oswiecim. You could go on enduring the hunger, the fatigue, the cold for month after month. You could struggle through your work and stagger under your beatings day after day.

You could nurse the wounds that never healed. You could permit your values to become so distorted that you would steal a piece of bread from a dying man without the slightest twinge of conscience, or whine like a spoiled child for a larger share of a pallet, or even beat to death a prisoner caught trying to escape. Yes, you could survive the paralysis of fear, degradation and hopelessness — all this — and still want to live!

And then some little trifle—like the letter that overstrained Jan's anxiety — would puff out the faint will to exist that had fluttered in your breast, just as a tree might stand up against the most violent storms only to totter and fall one day from the pressure of a gentle breeze. Thus worked the slow poison of Oswiecim, deteriorating the spirit even more than the body.

I knew Jan was feeling despondent, but I did not realize he was so desperate, until the day we were down in the fields by the southern boundary. We had worked down to the warning wire — a single strand of wire on which was hung a sign marked "Halt!" Beyond that was No-Man's Land — a strip of ground about a hundred yards wide extending to the electrified barbed-wire fence. There were watchtowers at frequent intervals along the fence all around the camp. Any prisoner seen between the warning wire and the outside fence was instantly fired on by the men in the watchtowers and by any other guards in the vicinity.

All at once, without a word to me or anyone else, Jan started to walk toward the fence. I called as soon as I saw what he was doing, but he did not turn back. The guards with our party yelled "Halt!" and started firing on him. Passing the warning wire he started to run in the direction of the watchtower — slowly at first, because it was then plain that he wanted all to see that he was making a deliberate and thoroughly hopeless break. His shoulders were back, his head was up — even from the back you could see his defiant expression that cried out, "Riddle me with bullets, you fools! Come on—kill me, hurry!"

And riddle him they did. The machine guns opened up, but on he ran, faster now and streaming blood. Still the spirit was master over the bullets that struck him again and again. Finally, as he reached the barbed-wire fence, he stumbled into it head first. Then he crumpled—and Jan was just a shattered mass of flesh.

When they tore his body loose from the fence there was no defiance in his face. Just a smile—a smile of profound relief. Jan had made good his escape.

"We must realize that the world is concerned about Oswiecim not because it has served as a prison for so many, nor because thousands of people have already been murdered there, and no one knows how many more may expect a similar fate. Primarily, the world is concerned with Oswiecim because of the moral problems it poses, because, as the tragic symbol of Nazi domination over Europe and Nazi inhumanity, it presents in a nucleus the problems faced by the community of oppressed European nations."—

From "Wolnosc" (Freedom), the oldest Polish underground labor paper, August 1943.

According to information from the Polish underground, up to July 194, 294,000 persons were executed in Oswiecim. The death toll rose to 667,161 for the period between September 1942 and August 1943. According to a report by the Very Reverend Paul Vogt, head of the Swiss refugee organization, the Fluchtlingshilfe, the executions of Jews in Oswiecim amounted to 1,715,000 during the two years ended April 15, 1944, as reported in the New York Times, July 6, 1944.

"The record written in blood at Oswiecim and institutions like it in the Nazi dominated countries

should be preserved to document the diabolical methods of Nazi suppression and warn the free men of the future against the tyranny which we allowed to rise and blight our time."—ELMER DAVIS, Director, Office of War Information

Chapter 12

Other Sources

Eva Kor is a survivor of the Holocaust. She and her twin sister Miriam, was subjected to torture and human experimentation by Josef Mengele at Auschwitz. Both her parents and two sisters were killed in the camp; only she and Miriam survived. Eva Kor founded the organization CANDLES ("Children of Auschwitz Nazi Deadly Lab Experiments Survivors"), through which she located 122 other living Mengele twins, as the experiment survivors came to be known. Kor is also known in a documentary called, *Forgiving Dr. Mengele.*

Here is a quote from Eva Kor about her experience in the cattle cars:

"We were crammed in a cattle car and there was barely any air to breathe. There were about 100 people with no room to sit, no food, no water, and the only air was supplied by four little windows at the top of the cattle car. So the air was not that fresh either. It was the end of May, during a stretch that was very hot. During the day, that wood and metal cattle car box was heating up. Thinking back, I have no idea how we survived the trip itself in that cattle car. The conditions themselves were already deadly. In other cattle cars several people died. I think in our cattle car there was one person who died but I am not 100 percent sure. There was one bucket in the corner. It had some sheets around it and I assume this is what was used for the toilet. But because we had very little to eat and drink in those four days, I did not need to use the facilities. So that is not what I would call "traveling." That is to me torture.

I need to explain our journey in that cattle car, because it is from my perspective unique. I have not heard a lot of people describe their own journey. We did not know where we were being taken. We were concerned and worried that we were not being taken to a labor camp in Hungary as the Hungarians told us when they put us in the cattle car at the ghetto. The train moved very fast. It seemed to me as a child that we were somehow "top priority." It would stop only for one reason, which seemed to me like refueling. I don't know what they were refueling on. Maybe it was steam, I don't know. Whenever they stopped, there was some kind of mechanical thing going on. There was no reason for them to stop for us, it was something they needed to keep the train going. That was my understanding - I could be wrong.

Anytime the train would stop, we would ask a question of the guard by our cattle car. Every single cattle car wagon had a booth by it, and in the booth was a guard with a machine gun. So we would ask the guard by our cattle car for water. We were very, very thirsty. The guard would always say, "Five gold watches." The grown-ups gathered the gold watches and passed them through the barbed wire windows. The guard would take a bucket of water and throw it from the ground through the window. I put my cup over my head hoping to catch some water. The truth is I never got more than a few drops. I don't believe anyone else did either. As that was happening, I wondered to myself, *Why are we asking for water and giving them gold watches, when the end result is we are not getting any water?* I never would have dared ask my parents why are we doing that. Now I understand that people who are scared to death do not verbalize their thoughts. They usually turn inward. Today I understand why we were doing it. It was our only way of getting some information of where we were being taken.

It was the end of the third day. The train stopped. We asked for water, and the answer came back in German. I was ten years old, but I instantly knew what had happened. We had crossed the border into occupied Germany (present-day Poland), therefore our Hungarian guards had changed to German. For me, that meant that the end was near and we were all going to be murdered. During the four years of occupation by the Hungarian army in my village, there were rumors that Jews were being taken to Germany to be murdered. We didn't know where, we didn't know how. But we had one hope that we were hanging onto: that we would never be taken to Germany. And that hope, as we crossed into occupied Germany, just vanished. Everybody in our cattle car was praying and crying, and the train moved on. It was next morning - about eight hours later. The train stopped again and we again asked for water. This time, there was no answer in any language. In my mind, I determined that this must be the final stop, and I was right.

We heard a lot of Germans yelling orders outside, then the cattle car doors slid open. Thousands of people from our cattle car and others poured out onto a little strip of land called the selection platform. That little strip of land that measures 85 feet long by 35 feet wide - I don't believe there is another strip of land like that anywhere on the face of this earth that has witnessed so many millions of people being ripped apart from their families forever.

As we stepped down onto the selection platform, my mother grabbed me and my twin sister Miriam by the hand. We were her youngest children. I believe she thought that as long as she could hold onto us, she could protect us. Everything was moving very fast. After about ten minutes, in my childish curiosity I looked around trying to figure out *what is this place?*, when I realized my two older sisters, Edit and Aliz, and my father had disappeared into the crowd. Never, ever did I see them again.

As we were holding onto mother, a Nazi was running and yelling in German, "Twins! Twins!" We did not volunteer any information. We had no idea what that place was and what worked there. He noticed Miriam and me because we were dressed alike and looked alike. He demanded to know if we were twins. My mother didn't know what to say because she didn't know if it was good. She asked, "Is that good?" The Nazi nodded yes. My mother said yes. At that moment, another Nazi came and pulled my mother in one direction. We were pulled in the opposite direction. We were crying. She was crying. All I remember is seeing her arms stretched out in despair as she was pulled away. I never even got to say goodbye to her. But I didn't really understand that this would be the last time I would see her. All that took thirty minutes from the time we stepped down from the cattle car. Miriam and I no longer had a family. We were all alone, and we had no idea what would become of us. And all that was done to us for one simple reason: because we were born Jewish, and I did not understand why that was wrong."

Heinrich Himmler was one of the most powerful men in Nazi Germany and one of the people most directly responsible for the Holocaust. Under Hitler's orders,

Himmler set up and controlled the Nazi Concentration camps. He was both Chief of German Police and Minister of the Interior, overseeing all internal and external police and security forces, including the Gestapo SS (Secret State Police).

Numerous books have already been published dealing with Himmler's concentration camps and the methods used in them. There is not space here to depict the camps and their cruelties in detail, but something must be said regarding the way Himmler employed these establishments for extorting and gagging public opinion and for intimidation.

In the book: Hitler's Last Days & Hitler's 12 Apostles: "And how did Himmler carry out this extortion? Quite simply: prisoners were martyred in such a way that their outcry was heard the world over. Here are a few brief facts, vouched for by thousands from personal experience, which show Himmler's measures in a proper light.

Those hostages, for instance, who after the 10th of November, 1938, were taken by train to the Dachau concentration camp, had to face a glaring light during the whole of their fifteen-hour journey in cattle trucks. If their eyes showed any inclination to close, or their heads to sink, they immediately received one or more truncheon blows on the head until they collapsed. They had hardly recovered their senses when they were forced to face the glare again. They were given nothing to eat or drink, were not allowed to stir from their places and were not permitted to ease nature. The road from the station to the Dachau concentration camp was intentionally strewn with sharp stones, and they had to traverse this on all fours, beaten incessantly by their escort. Some of the prisoners had already gone crazy on the journey, others had raving attacks and were shot; but their bodies were left in the trucks with the other prisoners.

In the prison itself these captives received only a thin drill suit with no overcoat, although it was the depth of winter. They had to stand, to report, for hours in snow, rain, and cold, bareheaded and in many cases without boots or shoes; chills, pneumonia, particularly rheumatism were the lesser consequences. Many perished after only a few days.

All this was quite regular and applied to all prisoners. It would be unbearable even to describe the punishments which were laid on these poor people for the slightest offense, and that oftentimes fabricated one. Relatives were made aware of all these horrors inflicted on fathers, husbands, and brothers, and when Himmler estimated that this oppression would suffice to open the frontiers of the rest of the world to these blameless victims of a raging bestiality he was right.

Here is another example of extortion and intimidation as brought into play in the K.Z.'s (the German abbreviation for the concentration camps):

On a freezing cold winter's day in January, 1939, a tiller's mate (Aryan, but Communist) who had been at work on new buildings escaped out of the camp. When he was found to be missing at evening roll call, all prisoners were ordered to assemble on the square in summer clothing as a punishment. For twenty-four hours, a whole night and a whole day, they had to stand motionless and at attention, exposed to icy winds. It was not until daybreak, after twelve hours of standing, that half an hour's rest was granted them, and this only after three of them had collapsed and died from cold and exhaustion. This method was intended to cure the prisoners of all further desire to attempt escape. It showed them that they would only bring suffering to their comrades, and an amazing bond of fellowship existed among them. (The escaped prisoner was captured in the woods after a few days and brought back to the camp, where he vanished, never to be seen again.)

How To Contact The Author

Originally published in 1944, A True Account Of Life in a Concentration Camp. Remade and translated by World War II Publishing from Reports, memoirs and accounts collected by the Polish Underground Survivors.

Glenn Langohr remade this book from the public domain to give a voice to the voiceless. If you would like to check out Glenn's other books on Amazon, they are available in kindle, print and audio book worldwide. He writes prison memoirs, prayer books and self help books, along with remade public domain works.

Dear reader,

It is with sincere gratitude that I would like to thank you for reading Oswiecim: Our Walk Into The Camp of Death Book 2 of Auschwitz: Frozen Memories of the Concentration Camps. I truly hope this book has been an eye opening experience. If you have enjoyed this book, **please consider being kind enough to leave a review on Amazon.** It would be helpful to other readers and me. Tap this link and scroll down about halfway on the left to where it says, want to leave a review~ If you can share it on Facebook, Twitter or anywhere else I thank you and will gift out a FREE kindle copy of one of my other books! Or, If you want one of my other books and can't afford it, I will gift you a kindle book. I write prison and drug war books, and prayer books. You can contact me at rollcallthebook@gmail.com or friend me on Facebook to keep up with updates and praise reports here~
https://www.facebook.com/glennlangohrcalifornia
Would you rather listen to my books? Here is a complete list of my audio books~
http://amzn.to/1aeliPs

God Bless You.

You can contact Glenn:
Author Page: http://www.amazon.com/-/e/B00571NY5A
Author Page UK: http://www.amazon.co.uk/-/e/B00571NY5A
Blog: http://www.audiobookprisonstories.com
http://rollcallthebook.blogspot.com/
Smashwords: http://www.smashwords.com/profile/view/lockdownpublishing.com
Twitter: https://twitter.com/#!/rollcallthebook

Printed in Great Britain
by Amazon